Conscience:
I Denounce Hate

WILLIAM J.

AZINA MEDIA
237 Flatbush Avenue, #187 Brooklyn, NY 11217

This is an original publication of AZINA MEDIA
PUBLICATIONS.

DEDICATION

I would like to dedicate this book to the 9 Charleston
victims
who lost their lives while serving God:

Rev. Clementa Pinckney
Rev. Daniel Simmons Sr.
Cynthia Hurd
Sharonda Singleton
Myra Thompson
Tywanza Sanders
Rev. Depayne Middleton-Doctor
Susie Jackson
Ethel Lance

FOREWORD

Let us all take the time to remember these nine wonderful people who devoted their lives to God.

The Rev. Clementa Pinckney was not only a pastor who preached at the AME church, but he was also a State Senator as well as a God-fearing man. You will be remembered.

The Rev. Daniel Simmons Sr. was a longtime pastor of the AME church. He was also a God-fearing man. You will be remembered.

Cynthia Hurd was a member of this wonderful AME church. She was also a devoted library worker who only wanted to help improve lives. She was also a God-fearing woman. You will be remembered.

Sharonda Singleton was a Reverend at Emanuel AME church. She was a speech therapist and a track coach as well as a God-fearing woman. You will be remembered.

Myra Thompson was a Bible study teacher who loved to spread God's word. She was also a God-fearing woman. You will be remembered.

Tywanza Sanders will be remembered as a hero. He wasn't just a person who made you smile, he was an uplifting servant of God. He was also a God-fearing man. You will be remembered.

Rev. Depayne Middleton-Doctor was a school administrator and a devoted servant of God. She was a leader and an enthusiastic singer at one point. She was also a God-fearing woman. You will be remembered.

Susie Jackson was a longtime member of the AME Charleston church. She was a devoted choir member and she was also on the usher board for the church. She was also a God-fearing woman who will be remembered.

Ethel Lance was a retired 70-year-old God-Fearing woman. She was a wonderful person who left a mark. You will be remembered.

As we take the time to remember these wonderful people, let us also take the time to make sure their deaths were not in vain. We must continue to spread God's word. The Devil comes in many shapes and forms and he's constantly looking for recruits. We, as believers in God must have enough faith to understand that battles are waged on many fields. We cannot lose faith simply because of one lost battle, when we as believers will always be tested. This tragedy should not hinder our faith. Instead, it should steel our resolve. Prestige is only gained when these battles fortify our weaknesses, hence, prepares us for war. Since the beginning of time, God's people, believers, followers, have always been made a martyr, yet we overcame and as his word spreads on, we shall overcome.

The Devil has no power over God's people, and as we remember these 9 lives lost in the Charleston massacre, we know the Devil had no power over them.

Fifty percent of all proceeds made from this book donated to:

Emanuel African Methodist Episcopal Church
110 Calhoun Street
Charleston, South Carolina
In remembrance of those nine lives lost on that dreadful day.

CHAPTER 1

Ryan paced back and forth in the dark barnyard, he couldn't believe what just transpired. Only several hours ago, him and his racist KKK cronies kidnaped a prominent black preacher. He wasted, beaten and subsequently denied his free will. Ryan just recently joined the clan on his 18th birthday and finally felt a part of something. For most of his life, he's been a sheltered loner who grew up on a farm. He was introduced to this way of life from his many searches of online acceptance. He now believed he found his calling, and this act only solidifies his place among the throng.

Mark finally came back to. However, his body felt out of sorts. He was unaware of his surroundings, considering a pillowcase was draped over his head. The last thing he remembered was leaving his church and being approached by a young white male with a clean shaven head. The guy asked him if he knew why he was there and Mark simply smiled before feeling a searing pain in the back of his head. That is as far as his memory would take him.

With his hands and feet bound he couldn't move, his only available senses were smell, taste, and sound. At the moment, he hears footsteps astir, he also smells a musty odor amidst as if he were near cattle, and once he licks his dry lips, he merely tastes salty blood. God help me! are his thoughts as he begins to recite a silent prayer. He's 42 years old with a loving wife and three grown children. He can only imagine what his family is going through, and from the worry, he adds them to his prayer as well.

After about 2 hours of silent torture, Mark gathers enough courage to speak. "Please sir," he humbly speaks out, "can you tell me what's going on."

The pacing stops and it gets eerily quiet. Mark shudders, anxiously waiting for a reply.

Ryan heard the man and couldn't believe he was awake, let alone alive. He thought his crew had beaten him to death, which was how bad they assaulted him. As he stands there looking at the beaten preacher who's hog-tied along with a pillowcase draped over his head, he begins to have a mix of emotions, and just to rectify his stance he simply says, "Shut up nigger!" Mark cringed as he revisits his past thoughts Please God, help me!

CHAPTER 2

24 Hours Later

Mark's humble abode is no longer humble. His wife along with two of his children, his eldest son who's twenty-two years old and his daughter whose 21 years old occupy the residence. His youngest son had yet to come home. However, there were concerned church members who were there to show their support. Mark's wife, Carylon had recently received a disturbing call from a racist white cult demanding, not a ransom but an ultimatum. She was told if the church wasn't burnt to the ground by their next day of worship, which happened to be 6 days away, her husband would be killed in a brutal fashion. She was also warned that if she contacted the police he would receive the same fate. With this knowledge, she feels stuck between a rock and a hard spot.

"Sister Carylon, everything's gonna be alright," the curly top deacon consoled, as he placed a concerned hand on her shivering shoulder, "why don't we all have a word of prayer," he offers. The group quickly held hands and bowed their heads.

5 minutes into their prayer, Mark's youngest son

Darryle, who recently turned eighteen burst in the house wide-eyed with bloodshot eyes, "Where the fuck is my dad!" he barked.

Everyone present looks up in mock disbelief at Darryle's brazen outburst. His mother is the first to speak, "Son, I understand your anger but please show some respect for the guests in this house," she pled, "we were in the middle of prayer when you came, now would you like to join us?"

Darryle scoffs, "Why the fuck would I be on my knees while my dad is being tortured! How bout you ask God that!"

Several guests are aghast at his lack of respect. Samson, Mark's eldest son quickly jumps in his little brother's face, and he could tell he's drunk, the liquor is clearly oozing off his pores, "How dare you come in this house and blatantly disrespect my mother like that."

Darryle chuckles, "She's my mother too, so get ya facts straight for you start mouthing off," is his sharp retort.

Samson stares at his little brother with disdain. He couldn't understand him sometimes. He even questioned if they were biological siblings, considering they were like night and day. Darryle was considered the black sheep of the family, and although no one ever said it, he could sense it. He always stayed in trouble at most times and didn't respect authority. He was the total opposite of his family, who were all church devoted Christians. Since Darryle became a teen he hated going to church, and when he was forced he made sure he made a spectacle. His family would be so embarrassed by his actions, his father Mark took a stance. He sat him down one day and had a heart to heart with him, or so he thought. He simply told his son that if he continued his ways the devil would trap him in his snares, and until he could show some respect for the church he didn't want him there. That was the last time Darryle ever stepped foot in a church.

Mariam, Mark's reserved daughter, jumps in the middle

of her brother's ensuing dispute, "Both of y'all need to calm down, our father is God know's where and you two fools got the nerve to pick a fight. He needs us right now more than ever, so Darryle, why don't you come and pray with us, we really need you."

"No, what you need to do is pray for them punk ass cracka's, cause I'm a kill 'em all, and I don't give a fuck who sort em out!" And with that, Darryle left the house followed by a slam of the door. His siblings, on the other hand, were not at all surprised.

CHAPTER 3

A burning cross with a melee of KKK members stood in the middle of a barnyard. The air was still, considering the late night in June. However, the heat emanating from the burning wood caused all members in their KKK robes to sweat profusely. In total, there stood twenty-one followers, twenty of them were dressed in all white with hoods on, resembling Casper the Friendly Ghost. The leader, who's apparently the odd member out is draped in a blue robe, and he's considered the Grand Dragon. This is their place of worship and at the moment the Grand Dragon is preaching rhetoric.

"Gentlemen," he carried on, "this is a day of great progress. We captured an important nigger preacher who was cancer to our cause, and now since we have him, this will be a great blow to the nigger community who plagues our pure existence!" Everyone cheers and hoots as if their team just won a championship, "Today my people, we are closer to our ultimate goal; one nation and nigger free!" The gathering erupts in a joyous rant that can be heard in the high heavens. After a moments time the leader raises his hand to silence the crowd, "People" he continues, "we must welcome one of our newest recruits, who played a major role in this righteous act, and for this he is now a full hooded member, Ryan, please step forward."

Ryan takes center stage with pride. He is finally apart of something and although he wasn't particularly fond of the KKK's actions, he was more than happy all the same. Growing up he was never around blacks, but he also wasn't taught to hate them. His family was a loving pair having recently been killed in a car crash. From that point, he felt more alone than ever, considering that was the only family he knew. But now it's his time and he plans to make the Grand Dragon proud.

The Grand Dragon embraced him in the secret brotherly hug, and the ensuing members followed suit. Although his face isn't visible, Ryan beams with delight.

"Ryan," The Grand Dragon begins, "You showed us that you are worthy of the cause. We now induct you as a full hooded member, and for our appreciation of your noble act of justice, we as one," He spreads his arms, "grant you the honor to kill the nigger preacher if our demands are not met."

The entire cult erupts in another fit of celebration. The Grand Dragon hugs Ryan again and whispers in his ear, "Make us proud son," he said, before raising Ryan's hand in the air as if he was the victor. Although he told Ryan he was a full pledge member, he had to pass one more test, he had to kill a black man, and that man was going to be the preacher, no matter if the demands were met or not. There was no way in the world the Grand Dragon would let a black man free, especially having already been entrapped in his snares.

CHAPTER 4

Darryle storms in the clubhouse where his gang members frequent.

He's wild-eyed with a deranged look etched on his face. His affiliate, Mack sees him and immediately perks up.

"Yo, what's popping Blood!" he addressed with morbid concern.

Darryle doesn't respond right away, he simply paces back and forth in another realm. The dwelling possessed a pool table, several game machines, and two couches, coupled with numerous red crates. The establishment is quite small, but its members don't seem to mind. There are currently fifteen people in attendance and everyone is occupied with one of the various activities. All parties present is an active gang member, they call themselves "Bloods" and rep the G-Shine set, and will die for what they believe in.

"Blaze," Mack called Darryle by his gang name, "what's popping?"

Pulled from his trance, he momentarily stares at Mack before he barks, "Some racist rednecks kidnaped my pops!"

Everyone present stopped what they were doing. You

could literally hear a mouse urinating on cotton as they all stared at Darryle not sure of what they just heard. "Say what now!" Mack spat.

"Man," Darryle placed his hands on his head, "these fuckin Crackas kidnaped my pops!" He repeats.

"Who, Pastor Mark?" One of the younger members blurted.

Darryle looks at the youngster as if he'd lost his marbles, "I only got one fuckin dad man!"

"My fault Blaze, it just sounds unbelievable," he admits.

"Well believe it!"

Mack speaks up, "So what you wanna do homie?"

Darryle doesn't think twice, "We bout to give these cracka's hell! Anybody white becomes a target," He looks around the room at all the grim faces," is y'all wit me?"

"Hell yeah!" Several younger members shout, anxious to get into some trouble.

"Hold up Blaze," Mack interrupts, as several members can be heard cocking their guns, "It sound like you tryna start a race war, why don't we run this by Pop Off first and see what he say," He tries to reason, referring to their leader who is considered their Godfather.

Darryle twists his face, "Man, we don't have time for-"

"Run what by me?" Pop Off barks as he enters the clubhouse.

Darryle, along with all his cohorts turns to look at their Godfather, who stood 5'9, dark skin in complexion with a muscular build. He possessed a stern face as if he was always serious, and commanded respect by any means necessary. As he stands there looking at Darryle, he figured he was the instigator who riled his pups up, considering he's the only one standing in the middle of the small room.

"Don't everybody speak at once," Pop Off barks, "run what by me?"

Every member present looks at Darryle, indirectly confirming Pop Off's suspicions. Darryle breathes hard as he stares at Pop Off, contemplating his words. "Basically," he begins, frustration clearly in his tone, "some racist ass cracka's kidnaped my pop and we bout to go find him."

"That's it"? Pop Off questioned.

"Pretty much! And while we looking for him, we plan to terrorize any and everything white!"

"The plot thickens," Pop Off spat, clearly being sarcastic, "So let me get this straight, a group of racist white people kidnapped your dad and you plan to go find him, but while you're on the way you plan to assault innocent white people as well?"

"I wouldn't call white people innocent, they-"

"So what would you call them?" he interrupts, "Matter fact, don't answer that," Pop Off said, as he finds a seat by the edge of the pool table, and tosses a Q-ball in his hand, "Answer this, do you know exactly who kidnapped your dad?"

"Well, the way I got it was, it's supposed to be the KKK."

Pop Off becomes thoughtful, as he fiddles with the Q-ball, "So, the KKK kidnaps your pop and notifies you?"

"Something like that, they spoke to my mom's."

"What're their demands?"

"They told her if she didn't burn the church down by Sunday, they were gonna kill him. They also said that if the cops were contacted they would kill him as well. So you see Pop Off, I have no choice."

"You always have a choice young-blood," Pop Off offered, "Now the way I see it, the cops are completely out the question. I find it hard to believe that they would knock down doors looking for your father. My other concern is regarding the KKK, you see, there are countless racist cults that reside here in the south, so it would be hard to pinpoint the actual group that kidnaped your father. Our best bet is to put some eyes and ears out there because I know for a fact your family not burning that church down."

"And why the fuck not!" Darryle barked, "If they

don't, my pops is dead."

"Two reasons," Pop Off said, as he throws up two fingers, "first of all, that church is a historical landmark, now it might come up for a topic of discussion but the elders would never agree to those terms. Secondly, the KKK doesn't plan to let your father live, ultimatum or not, it's not in their nature."

"Then fuck it! I'll burn the church down myself, and we'll see if they let him live," Darryle spat.

"Listen to yourself Blaze," Pop Off reasoned, "you talking about burning a historical church down, what sense does that make?"

Darryle sighs hard, "Then we'll kidnap a white preacher and give them cracka's hell!"

Pop Off angrily shakes his head, "Are you tryna start a fuckin race war, Blaze?"

"They already started one!"

Pop Off abruptly stands to his feet, "That's not what we stand for! You sound like a hate monger! In case you forgot, let me remind you what "BLOODS" stand for; Brotherly Love Overrides Oppression Destruction in Society. It's that simple Blaze, we don't go around and attack innocent white people or any people for that matter. Now I understand you're angry, but don't let your anger turn to hate if we practiced that shit we would be no better than them, would you agree?"

Darryle didn't want to agree, but Pop Off was right, he couldn't go around hating a race for what some ignorant supremacist did. "You right Pop Off, I wasn't thinking."

"Youngblood, you have a fire in you that burns endlessly, and that is what drew me to you, just channel your anger in the right direction, not towards innocent people." Pop Off then addresses the group, "I want everybody on the street asking questions, being observant and staying alert, we got a pastor to find, and when we find the perpetrators that's the people we give hell, let's move out Bloods!"

CHAPTER 5

Mark has been captive for the past twenty-four hours. Still bound with a pillowcase over his head, he has yet to know his whereabouts. At the moment, he has to urinate as his appendix feels as though it's about to explode. He's been praying all night long, asking God to spare his life. His captor has been gone for the last 8 hours, and he's hungry, he feels sick and his body still aches. Perspiration trickles down his face, as shuffling can be heard close by. Ryan opens the door to the barn-house and as expected he sees the pastor laying in the same position in the exact same spot. Good, he thought, and right before he turns to leave, the pastor speaks.

"Please, can I relieve myself?" .He asked.

Ryan heard the pain in his voice and feels somewhat sorry for the man, he could only imagine what he was going through. Ryan locates a metal pot, unbinds the pastor's hands, but keeps his feet bound. "Here's a pot, handle your business and make it quick," he said, silently watching.

The pastor literally urinated for four minutes, like a racehorse. Damn Ryan thought he really had to go. Once done, he retrieves the pot and before he could step off, the pastor speaks again.

"Please, can I have a sip of water?"

Ryan doesn't speak, he simply leaves the barn, and several minutes goes by before he returns with a cup of water.

Moments later Mark's pillowcase is removed. He blinks several times before his eyes can adjust to his surroundings. He looks around and realizes he's inside of a barn. Wooden ledges are barricaded around the spacious setting. Horse stables are to his right and left with no horses in sight. He finally notices he's lying on mud and old hay. The lighting is dark and the ceiling is high. At this point, he feels like cattle. When he peers ahead, he sees his captor for the second time, holding a cup of water. This is the same kid who approached me at my church he thought.

Ryan stares at the preacher and feels even sorrier for him. His face is almost unrecognizable, his right eye is swollen shut, his lips have swelled tremendously from the trauma, and bruises can visibly be seen around his neck, coupled with a few lumps on his head. The pastor looks beaten and weak, so Ryan quickly places the cup to his mouth and is taken aback by the way he lapped up every drop.

Mark breathes out a sigh of satisfaction once his thirst is quenched. He could go for another round, but he doesn't want to push his luck. As of now he realizes he's being held for whatever reason, he doesn't know. To show his gratitude he meekly smiles, "Thank you son, and God Bless you for the water."

Ryan doesn't respond, he simply heads out as his conscious is having a battle from within.

CHAPTER 6

At the moment, Carylon is an emotional wreck, her husband has now been gone for 48 hours and they're only 4 days away from worship. She's been praying so much her knees are sore. What kind of sick people was she dealing with, and did they actually think she would burn the church down. She surely was considering it, she would almost do anything to keep her husband alive.

"Children, what am I left to do," she wept, as her son places a comforting hand on her shoulder.

"Mom, all we have to do is pray and ask God to show us the way," he reassures.

"He's right mom," Mariam joins in, "we don't want to make any rash decisions."

Carylon sighs, unsure of her thoughts. She calmly takes a seat and closes her eyes, as flashes of her loving husband invade her mind. She sees his warm smile, envisions his handsome face, and hears his baritone voice~ the pulpit. They've been married for twenty years and they've been devoted to God well before they consummated their marriage. Was this just about the church? It had to be, she thought. Her husband couldn't possibly have any enemies. He only did God's work, he helped at soup kitchens for the homeless, he assisted with kids who had autism, he sponsors a youth basketball team for teens fifteen and under. He's also a State Rep. This man is truly a beautiful person who only helps people. It was that same compassion that attracted Carylon to him in the first place.

"Mom!" Samson called.

Jarred from her thoughts, she reluctantly opens her eyes. She wanted to keep daydreaming, but she knew reality would come knocking soon enough. "Yes sweetie," she answered.

"We only have 4 days before they make their move, so I thought that we should maybe get some volunteers to form a search party," He said.

She sighs again, wearily staring at her son. She sees the pain in his eyes, confusion of the unknown. She then looks to her daughter who's just as distraught, the only difference being, Mariam's emotions have a mind of their own, as tears endlessly slide down her face. They're hurting and there's not a damn thing she can do about it. At this point, she hates to be the torchbearer, but with both of her offspring looking to her for guidance, she stands to her feet.

"Children," she begins, "we have to go see the elders of our father's church and convince them to burn it down," She said, almost apologetically. Both siblings look at each other, before looking back to their mother.

As she stares at them, she sees shock, confusion, and a slight semblance of understanding all bottled into one expression. They both nod their heads simultaneously, and she in turn nods back, before closing her eyes again, Please God show me the way she silently prays, hoping God doesn't strike her down for even speaking of such blasphemy.

CHAPTER 7

The night is slowly winding down as both Mack and Darryle sit in a late model Buick parked outside of a sports bar. With Mack being the designated driver, he picked this part of town where 95% of the residents are Caucasian. They've been sitting there for the past two hours quietly observing everyone who entered and exited. It appeared as if they were on a stakeout, and as the sun sluggishly dies, so does Darryle's patience.

"Why I get the feeling we wasting valuable time sitting outside of this stupid ass sports bar!" He spat.

Mack doesn't answer, he simply keeps his eyes glued to the entrance. Several minutes later, Darryle blows out hot air, and as the sun dies so does his patience. He pulls his gun from his hip and places it on his lap before expressing his thoughts, "The next cracka that step outta that bar getting snatched, then interrogated, how that sound?"

"It sounds like you ain't listen to nothing Pop Off said. Now I understand your anger but you gotta have patience Blaze."

"Patience!" Darryle repeated, like it was a dirty word, "My pop got 4 days left before them racist mutha fucka's hang him from a tree, I could care less about patience, we need to make a move, and soon!"

Mack remains silent as he appears to be deep in thought, and this only keeps Darryle talking.

"What would you do if somebody kidnaped ya pops and told you, you only had six days before they kill his ass? Shit! I'm willing to bet my life you wouldn't be sitting here outside of a sports bar playing Inspector Gadget."

"Hold up Blaze, I think we got something," Mack said, as a white male stumbles out the bar, visibly drunk.

Darryle perks up and grips his gun, before hastily grabbing the door handle.

Mack grabs his arm, "Hold up Blaze, what you doing?"

Darryle looks at Mack with his face twisted, "You know what I'm doing! I already told you the next mutha fucka that come outta that bar getting snatched!"

Mack shakes his head, "Just relax Blaze, we gone follow this dude and see where that leads us."

Darryle sighs again. "Man, this mutha fucka so drunk he might lead us into a ditch, and you talking bout following his ass. To be honest Mack, I really don't see no sense in that."

"That's because you not seeing what I'm seeing."

Darryle strains his eyes intently staring at the white man, who struggles to locate his keys, as he staggers outside of his red pick-up truck. "What the fuck is you looking at to make you wanna follow this clown."

Mack smiles, "Look again and check out that tattoo on his arm."

Darryle leans forward in his seat to get a better view, "What? It's just a flag."

"Not just any flag, it's the Confederate flag!"

"And?"

"And!" Mack repeated in disbelief, "You must don't know your history Blood."

"What about my history?"

"For starters, that flag represents hatred. You see, back in the day you had the North versus the South. They went to war to abolish slavery, and the North was fighting for us, black people. But here in the South, these racist mutha fucka's wanted to keep us segregated forever, they pretty much viewed black people as less than human beings, and that flag that dude got on his arm was the same flag that the South used to represent they punk asses."

"Oh yeah," Darryle said, clearly intrigued, "I be seeing that flag hanging up all over." He then becomes thoughtful for a moment, "As a matter fact, that same fuckin flag hanging up at the courthouse!"

Mack chuckles, "I know, and the crazy thing is, them punks lost the war, but they still believe in that flag, you know why right?"

Darryle nods his head, "Yeah I know why, them cowards still believe in racism."

Mack smiles, "So you see, racism still exists, but here in this new age it 1 s not as open. These racist mutha fuckas can't get away with the same shit that they could back in the day, now it's controlled to an extent. But do you know the most racist shit that's going on right now, besides locking up so many black men?"

"Killing us?"

"You damn right! The worst thing they could've did was give a racist white man a badge and a gun. In they twisted mind, they think they got a license to kill all black people, and them mutha fucka 1s been getting away with that shit for so long, it was almost legal. All a cop had to say was he had a weapon, or he tried to reach for theirs, and the case was closed. But thank the powers that be for modern technology, with all these cell phones with cameras and shit, they can't kill us and tell lies like they used to. Lately them racist mutha fucka's been getting caught, and now they being held accountable, for the simple fact that the country is literally in an uproar."

"Damn! That's some deep shit," Darryle acknowledged.

"Naw, this some deep shit. Do you know what "nigger" means?"

"Yeah, it mean a lot of shit, but it basically means an ignorant black man."

"You right on point, but ask a racist white person why do they hate blacks, you know what they gone tell you?"

"Not really."

Mack chuckles, "I don't know either, but what I do know, is that they gone tell you some ignorant shit. So who's really the nigger?"

Darryle laughs, "That's a good point," he admits, as he sees the white man finally get in his truck, "Yo Mack, dude just got in the truck."

Mack starts the car up, "Good, let's see where this racist mutha fucka take."

CHAPTER 8

Mother Nature decided to cry as the downpour quelled the molten earth. The incessant rain pelts maul on the barn's roof in an off-beat rhythm. Still bound, Mark is uncomfortably on his knees in deep prayer. He seemed to block out the heavy gusts that collaborated with the thunderstorm. The wind whipped and rocked the wooden barn house with such force, he wondered if the wood would hold. Hence his hindered sight he couldn't decipher the hour or day for that matter, he simply prayed that his captor would release him or at least feed him some type of food. His injuries coupled with his lack of malnourishment spurs him to pray out loud in hopes that God will literally hear his pleas.

"The spirit of the Lord is upon me," he pleads, "because you Lord have appointed me to preach good tidings to the poor; You have sent me to heal the brokenhearted, to proclaim liberty to the captives, and the openings of the prison to those who are bound; To proclaim the acceptable year of the Lord, and the day of vengeance of our God."

Mark is so moved he starts to cry, deep sobs, as if he'd lost a loved one. The pillowcase draped over his head is tear stained, from agony, hunger pains, anxiety, all bottled into one heap. As he somewhat gathers himself, he carries on, "Please God, forgive my enemies, for they know not that they have sinned. I ask you to cover them in your blood, for hate is detested in your kingdom. Show them the way Lord, and have mercy on their souls."

He cries harder, as his emotions spiral out of control. His knees can no longer bear his weight, and he crumbles to the surface. With his hands and feet bound nothing breaks his fall but thank God for the rain, which leaked through the roof of the old barn, thus softening the mud and hay that lay beneath him, diminishing the impact. As he lays, broken and battered, he still weeps an everlasting cry.

Ryan is frozen in place, having entered moments ago while the pastor was praying. Tears are streaming down Ryan's guilt-ridden face. He couldn't believe the pastor would actually pray for him and his cohorts, and even forgive them. As he stands there, he's overrun with compassion, as he saw the pastor fall to the surface. Ryan's conscious is on the brink, why did this man have to be so holy. He wished they had kidnaped a black man who was angry, maybe then he would feel better. Whatever the case, he didn't believe this man deserved this.

I have to get ahold of myself, he tries to convince himself. He wouldn't dare let the Grand Master catch him bawling his eyes out for a black man. He quickly wipes his sullen face and tries to remain indigenous, his only hang-up is trying to hate this man, who did absolutely nothing but be black. I'll come around, he thought, as he heads toward the preacher.

In the midst of his soft sobs, Mark feels the nudge of a boot to his ribs, not too hard but applied with enough pressure to gain his attention. Although denied sight, Mark shudders from fear of the unknown.

"Hey," Ryan barks, "I got some food for you."

God is good, are the pastors thoughts, as he musters

enough strength to hoist himself to his knees, "Thank you." Mark said before he even received anything.

Ryan removes the pillowcase and unbinds his hands. The pastor stretches his arms in the air and is somewhat relieved. He blinks several times giving his eyes a chance to adjust. The atmosphere is dark as the surface is damp. Mark looks at his captor and sees a brown Burger-king bag in his hand. He meekly smiles as Ryan passes it over. Mark tears open the bag which only contains a hamburger. Before he dives in, he briefly closes his eyes and silently gives thanks for the food he's about to receive.

"You gotta hurry up and eat that," Ryan spat, "I was only told to feed you bread and water!"

"Okay," The pastor drawls, with a mouthful.

Exactly ten seconds later, Mark is finished. When he hands over the empty bag, Ryan balls it up and eases it in his pocket. He then pulls out a Deer Park bottled spring water and passes it to the pastor. Mark's eyes light up as he guzzles the H2-D.

"Ease up," Ryan said, "I'm leaving for the day and you might get thirsty later on."

Mark levels the plastic bottle and stares at Ryan through pained eyes, "What's your name?" He asked.

Ryan stands there contemplating if he should answer the question. He doesn't give it much thought and several seconds later he binds the pastor's hands and proceeds to place the pillowcase over his head.

"Please man," Mark pleads, "Can you explain to me what's going on, I beg you."

Ryan halts, he clearly heard the ache in his voice, and his conscious won't allow him to leave, at least without an explanation. "Alright," he says, as he looks down at the pastor, "Three days ago you were kidnapped and my people contacted your people to l e t them know to burn your church down by Sunday, and you'll be free."

"I don't understand..." Mark said, "why would... who are your people if you don't mind me asking." "Well, I'm with the KKK!'"

Mark nods. He somewhat understood his dilemma, however, as he stares at Ryan, he sees nothing but a confused kid who doesn't really have his heart into it. Mark could tell the kid had some type of compassion, just from the simple fact that he gave him a hamburger and told him to hurry up. It was as if the kid didn't agree with only feeding him bread and water, and that small show of empathy motivates his next question. "Why are you doing this?"

"I just told you, man," he said, reaching for the pillowcase.

"Hold up, wait, please man, just hear me out, I have a wife and three wonderful children, I'm a God-fearing man and I... I..." Mark starts crying before he can finish his spiel.

Ryan's stomach drops, at this point he feels terrible. He'd never seen a grown man cry before, and in this case this man committed no crime. "I'm sorry man, about your family and all, but I gotta go." He places the pillowcase over his head, relieved he didn't cry himself, as he was clearly on the verge.

"Can you tell me your name, please," Mark spoke in a soft voice.

"It's Ryan!"

"Ryan, if you don't mind me asking, before you go I would like to have a word of prayer with you, I'll make it quick."

Ryan heaves out a sigh, and to be honest, he didn't see no harm in it, "I'm listening."

"Alright, before I begin, just place your hand on my shoulder, if you don't mind."

Ryan is only several feet away, and considering the pastor couldn't see him, he saw no harm in that request either. He takes the few steps and places a nervous hand on the pastor's shoulder before Mark begins.

"Behold, the Lord's hand is not shortened, that it

cannot save; nor his ear heavy, that it cannot hear. But your iniquities have separated you from your God; And your sins have hidden his face from you so that he will not hear. For your hands are defiled with blood, and your fingers with iniquity;

At this point, Ryan is touched. It seems as if God is talking directly to him.

"No one calls for justice, nor does any plead for truth. They trust in empty words and speak lies; they conceive evil and bring forth iniquity. They hatch viper's eggs and weave the spider's web; He who eats of their eggs dies, and from that which is crushed a viper breaks out. But the Lord will arise over you Ryan, and his glory will be seen upon you. You are a good man, and God knows your heart. Lord!" he said, with an ache in his voice, "Place your hands on this saint, steer his mind away from iniquity, close his ears from evil rhetoric. Save this young man so he can dwell in your kingdom forever. As I end this prayer I want you to touch his conscious, touch his soul, and as you have forgiven us for our sins, I forgive you Ryan, in Jesus name we pray, Amen!"

"Amen," Ryan muttered, as the tears silently came.

Silence attacked the stale air, and before another word could be spoken, Ryan scampered out, thinking about God touching his conscious.

CHAPTER 9

Wednesday 72 hours later

It is midday in the middle of June. The sun having already vaporized the drenched streets from the previous onslaught the day before makes it appear as if it's another beautiful day. For the church leaders at this historical house of worship, it is anything but beautiful. The devil has somehow found his way inside of these God-fearing church members lives and at the moment the elders along with several deacons discuss the future of their holy sanctuary.

"This is absurd Sister Carylon," one elder spat, "you can't possibly expect us to consider a request on account-"

"What!" Carylon abruptly stands to her feet, "on account of my husband being kidnaped, who, by the way, runs this church!" She looks at all 10 faces around the room with bloodshot weary eyes. To her, they all look smug, but truth be told they were just as hurt.

"Lets everybody settle down now," the deacon said, as he forced a concerned hand on Carylon 1s stiff shoulder, "Sister Carylon, we all feel your pain and we truly do understand your frustrations but do you honestly think your husband, who is our pastor, would want this?" The deacon asked as all parties stare at Carylon with sorrowful eyes.

Carylon is emotionally drained, and to be honest with herself, she knew very well her husband would not even entertain such a request. To burn God's house down on account of the devil's demands was absurd. But what was she left to do? Her husband, who she's been married to for over twenty years and who she happens to have three children by, is kidnaped with his life on the line. She feels as though she's stuck between a rock and a hard place. Overrun with agony and worry she flops back in her seat and cries for the life of her husband.

Her pain is heartfelt around the room as everyone huddles around to console her tormented soul. They all gather hands creating a circle with her in the middle.

"Dear Lord," the deacon begins, "We're gathered here today in this holy matrimony. We ask that you soothe Sister Carylon's soul, bring her husband back in one piece, our loving pastor. He is a good man, who helps the community, feeds the homeless, and cares for the sick. He is your vessel who you called to lead us, lead this wonderful church, which is your house. God, we ask that you return our pastor, Sister Carylon's husband, your vessel. Bring him out of the whale of Jonah, for he is like Job. Have mercy on his soul Lord, for we forgive his captors for they know not their sins. Intervene Lord, show us your mercy. Touch our souls, touch Sister Carylon's soul, watch over her beautiful children, and bring their father home. Praise God!" he finally shouts, as everyone murmurs to egg him on, "Yes Lord, have mercy on our souls. Gathered here today we are at your mercy, show us the way and release your vessel from the devil's hand as only you know how. As I close out this prayer I ask that you keep Sister Carylon covered in your blood, in Jesus name we pray, Amen."

"Amen," the entire room repeats.

Carylon is no longer crying. That prayer touched her soul, revamped her spirit, as only God can do. Everyone in the room hugs her one by one, and she in turn hugs them back. Although it looks bleak right now she really believes she'll get her husband back, somehow she can feel it.

CHAPTER 10

"Damn Mack," Darryle spat, "this dude been driving for the past hour. You sure his drunk ass ain't lost?"

"Might be," Mack said, peeping his surroundings, "but check out all this empty land out here."

"I see. For a mutha fucka to live out here, they gotta have money."

"Not necessarily! Being as though this is the country, a lot of this land was passed down from generation to generation, so you know what that mean."

"What?"

"Shit, a generation ago black people ain't have no money, and right now we talking about 2 generations ago. The bottom line is, this land is owned by white people and more than likely this shit was passed down from their forefathers. Back in the day I'm willing to bet that our ancestors worked in these fields."

"Damn! That's deep."

"Naw, it ain't deep, it's real. Now I'm not telling you this shit to make it seem like I hate white people, cause I don't."

Darryle contorts his face, "Even after what they did to us back in the day? You serious!"

"Dead serious! But Im'a never forget what they did to our people, but I'm not gone hold it against all white people either. If I did, that would make me a racist. Are you a racist?"

Darryle becomes thoughtful, as he ponders Mack's question. "Put it this way, I hate those mutha fucka's that kidnaped my Pops!"

"As you should, but do you hate the entire white race?"

"I can't say I do."

"And you know why, right?"

"Why?"

"It's not in our nature. Generally, in order for us to hate a mutha fucka, they would have to do something to us. And to be completely honest with you, we as black people hate each other more than anything. We wasn't born that way, we was taught that way."

"By who?"

"This vicious racist mutha fucka named Willie Lynch!"

"Who the fuck is that?"

Mack chuckles. "Where you think the word lynching came from!"

"Oh yeah! "

"That was one diabolical mutha fucka. But still, we can't use that as an excuse, we gotta break the cycle ourselves."

"How we do that?"

"Simple. First we gotta stop killing each other."

Darryle nods in agreement.

"That's another story for another time. Right now we bout to see what's up with this clown." Mack said as he watched their mark park his truck on a square mound of terrain, specifically designed for that purpose.

The stars shined bright on this night, as the full moon displayed all its glory. Being so high in the country it seemed as if the stars were in arms reach. The slight breeze from the late hour made the June heat bearable, so both Mack and Darryle patiently waited in the car for the guy to enter his abode. However, he never stepped foot inside of his spacious house, he entered a gated fence directly beside it, before completely disappearing.

"Damn, where you think he went?" Darryle quipped.

"It look like a backyard, but this what we gone do, since this the only visible house for the next mile we gone creep behind his truck, and on my count we gone slide in that gate. "

"Say no more," Darryle agreed, while checking his gun.

Several seconds later they both trot to the back of the truck in a crouched position. Once there, they duck down before drawing their guns. As the crickets chirp, Darryle sees something that vexes him.

"Ain't this about a bitch!" He spat.

"What's that?" Mack asked as he peeked around the truck.

"This punk mutha fucka even got the flag on his license plate!"

"The Confederate flag?"

"Yeah, look."

"Man fuck that flag right now, we bout to see what this joker up to, you ready?"

"Born! "

Still in a crouched position, they slowly walk to the gate, and once there, country music can be heard along with several voices.

"You hear that shit?" Darryle whispered.

"Yeah I hear it. So this what Im'a do, Im'a creep over there and peek behind the house, make sure you keep your eyes on me cause when I give you the signal, come, until then stay put."

"1 got you."

Mack quietly opens the gate and makes his way to the back of the house. Not even 5 seconds pass before he runs back with a look of horror on his face.

"What's up Mack?"

"Man, let's get the fuck outta here." He barked, still en

route towards the car.

Bringing up the rear, Darryle is clearly confused, but as he passes the truck he gets a bright idea. He fishes a marker from his pocket and doubles back towards the license plate.

"Come on Blood!" Mack barked, as he watched his partner doodle on the back of the truck.

Moments later, Darryle hastily enters the car and Mack quickly drives off, burning rubber in the process.

"Damn Mack! You ran outta that yard like you saw a ghost or something, what the fuck was that about?"

"Man, you do not wanna know."

"Try me."

"Put it this way, I saw 4 naked white men, need I say more!"

Darryle bursts out laughing.

"Man, that shit ain't funny!" Mack spat, "and besides, what the fuck did you write on that truck?"

Once Darryle gets his laughter under control, he responds, "I crossed that flag out and wrote "Fuck the Confederate flag!"

Mack chuckles, "Now that's some funny shit!"

CHAPTER 11

It's high noon and the sun is at its peak. The country roads are smooth as a late model Chevy Buick coasts towards the State store. Ryan, along with his KKK brother are the occupants and at the moment these two are en route to purchase enough liquor to get a whale drunk. They have an upcoming KKK rally tomorrow and Red's, the designated driver plans to go out inebriated.

"So," Red's begins, "how does it feel to be a full hooded member?" He asked, with a gratifying smile on his face.

Ryan becomes thoughtful, as he ponders his answer. "What can I say...? I'm just happy to be a part of the Clan."

"You're not just a part of the Clan, you are now a part of greatness, and on top of that your initiation act was a powerful blow that will be talked about for years."

"I didn't know that."

"Don't worry Ryan, you're still a new boot. I just wish that was my initiation act when I became a Clan member over twenty years ago."

"Wow!" Ryan said, in disbelief, "You've been a Clan member for twenty years?"

"You damn right I been! But the thing is, I hated niggers all my life."

"Why is that?"

"What kind'a question is that?"

"Well, I'm just curious as to why you started hating black people."

"Niggers you mean!" He spat in disgust.

"Yeah, yeah, niggers I meant."

"It's simple! They don't belong. Those vermin are animals, and back in the day they were born with tails."

Ryan looks at Red's, "Are you serious?"

"Very!"

Ryan knew people were sick, he just didn't know people were sick like Red's, but the more he stared at him, the more convinced he became.

"You see Ryan, I notice that baffled look on your face, but once you kill that nigger preacher, your conscious will be clear of doubt."

"Hold up now, I thought the Grand Dragon said if they burned the church down, I wouldn't have to kill him."

Red's chuckled, "If you didn't actually think we would let that nigger walk, did you?"

"Well, the Grand Dragon-"

"I don't care what the Grand Dragon said, you and I both know that's a dead nigger. To be honest, you should be honored to kill that nigger."

Ryan didn't know what to think, but that didn't stop him from voicing his thoughts. "So the church doesn't even matter?"

"We could care less about the church, or him being a preacher for that matter. Shit, I burnt down a nigger church as an act of my initiation. Once I did that, I earnt my place, the only thing I didn't like was the fact that there was not one nigger in there when I did it. But you Ryan, are really gonna make a difference. You see, that nigger is not just a pastor, he's also a State Senator with a powerful voice, that's why we gon' kill him."

Ryan is in shock, this man is not only a preacher helping the community, but he's also a State Senator.

"Is there a problem?" Red's asked once he noticed the incredulous look on Ryan's face.

Jarred from his thoughts, he gives a simple answer, "Not at all."

Red's smiles, "That's the spirit, all you-" He stops in mid-sentence once he realizes the cops are behind him with their sirens wailing, "Fuck is this about," he mumbled to himself.

As Ryan hears the sirens, he looks in the rearview and sees the patrol car trailing them. Red's quickly pulls over with a nonchalant look on his face, as if this is the everyday norm.

Once the cop exits the car, Ryan sees a white man with a pair of shiny knee high boots laced up to the neck. As he strolls his way toward their car, Ryan's heart starts beating double time. Red's calmly rolls his window down.

"How do you do officer," Red's greets.

The cop has a cowboy hat on, as a shadow covers half of his face. The only thing visible is the apparent scowl he wears along with his right hand clutching the butt of his gun, that's snugly nestled in his leather holster. "Im'a need both you boys to step outta this car," he barked, "this here vehicle has been reported stolen."

Oh shit, Ryan thought, I don't want to go to jail!

"Officer, I would step out if I could, but my partner here has a bomb strapped to his chest and he told me if I don't follow his orders he's gonna blow me up." Red's explained.

Ryan couldn't believe his ears, and before he could wrap his thoughts around the severity of the situation, the cop speaks.

"Young man, is this true?" He spat, as he unsnaps his holster.

Ryan is shook, "Um... I... uh-"

The cop along with Red's burst out laughing, and before Ryan caught the joke he grabbed the door handle, two seconds away from bolting.

"Bill, did you see the look on his face when you

unsnapped your holster," Red's quipped with humor.

"Did I!" Bill fires back, "That poor kid probably shit his pants," he then leans in the driver side window to peer at Ryan, "Son, you ain't shit ya pants now did you?"

"No sir officer."

Bill shoots a curious eye at Red's, "Where you find this here kid at Red, I've neva known you to be hanging around with quirky children."

Red's chuckles, "Ain't nothing quirky about this kid here Bill, he the one who got that nigger preacher foe us."

"Say it ain't so!" Bill said, clearly impressed. He then extends his hand towards Ryan, "I need to shake your hand son that was a noble act you did there. Now I just hope that body-cam shit die down so I can keep getting away with my dirt. Lord knows I done did enough shit to land me under the jail," he admits.

"You ·and me both," Red's seconds.

"Where you headed at anyhow, Red?"

"To the State store. You know we got a rally tomorrow."

"Yeah, I got the memo. Im'a try to make it this time around if duty don't call."

"You might wanna make this one Bill, we might just kill that nigger preacher that night."

"Then you can count me in. I wouldn't miss that for the world. Just make sure you save me a drink, we all know how you get."

Red's chuckles, "Im'a try," he joked, "just do your job and keep our here streets nigger free."

Bill salutes Red's with his hat, "Don't I always!"

"Yes, you do."

"Alright now, Im'a leave you two boys to it, and Red, I'll see you tomorrow," He said, as he proceeds to his patrol car.

"Looking forward to it Bill," Red's then looks at Ryan, "Don't look so surprised, everybody in this here part of town is like us.

Ryan nervously smiles as his thoughts swirl, what in the

world have I gotten myself into?

CHAPTER 12

With only 2 days until the deadline nerves are on edge. Carylon, along with her children, Mariam and Samson sit in their living room with worried faces. They just wrapped up another session of prayer and it seems as if they're no closer to getting Mark back.

"So," Samson begins, "the elders won't agree to burning the church down, huh?"

Carylon heaves a sigh, as she stares at her worried son, "Baby, its a little complic--"

He sighs as well, "Please mom, just give me a straight answer!"

"The answer is no, Samson. The elders will not agree to such nonsense, and I don't blame them!"

Mariam cocks her eye at her mother, "You don't blame them?"

Samson joins in, "Yeah mom, why not?"

She offers a weak smile as only a concerned mother would, "The devil has no voice in this house or God's house for that matter. His demands are only met from his worshipers and followers. We on the other hand," she looks at both of her children, "are Saints of the Lord, and we do as he says, and only him," she explained with certainty, "this is nothing but another ploy from the devil to claim one of God's sanctuary." ·

Mariam nods in agreement, but Samson isn't so understanding, "Mom," he begins, "we gon' have to figure out something. We could potentially be fatherless within the next 2 days, and if they don't allow us to burn the church down and these devil's wind up killing our father, which is your husband, would you ever forgive yourself?"

"Honey," she breathes out, "I have faith in God, I have enough faith to believe that he will deliver your father whether it be here on earth," she then points toward the ceiling, "or up there in heaven, he will be delivered."

"Mom," he whines in a shaky voice, "how could you say something like that?"

Carylon known her son long enough to know when he's on the verge of tears, and as he stands there with glossy eyes and quivering lips, she wraps him in her arms as he cries on her chest. This moment takes Carylon back countless years. She could remember a time when he was a curious child who would always fall and get hurt. He would do the same thing, run to his mother and bawl his little eyes out, and she would tell him the same thing she's about to tell him now, "It's okay sweetie," she soothes, "I'm here."

As Mariam looks at her brother fall apart, she has to restrain herself from doing the same. Watching this heartbreaking moment only spurs her to join in on the hug, and when she does, she suddenly gets a bright idea.

"Hold up y'all," she sang, now standing at arm's length, "Being as though we only have two days left it can't hurt if we contact the police, maybe they can help."

Carylon becomes thoughtful as she continues to hold her son, and before long she speaks her mind, "Pass me that phone, child!"

CHAPTER 13

"Look at these two hillbillies right here," Mack spat.

"I see em," Darryle concedes, as he watched them load cases of liquor into a late model Chevy, "it look like they bout to get pretty drunk, what's the crime in that?"

"They racist Blood! That mutha fucka right there," he points at the older one with the red beard, "is a certified racist!"

"How you know?"

"That clown got a Swastika tattoo on his elbow, that I s how I know."

"I don't know Mack," he said unconvinced, "you see where the last tattoo you saw, landed us."

"Man, I'm telling you!" Mack bangs his fist on the steering column, "that mutha fucka can't hide it! He got the eyes, the face, he even got that shiny bald ass head, that I would love to lick my black ass hand, and smack the shit out of!"

Darryle bursts out laughing, "Man you funny as shit."

"Man, I'm serious as shit! Just look at his face."

Darryle peers harder, "Yeah, he do look angry at the world."

"He ain't just angry at the world, he angry of the fact that us black people in it."

"Then what about his protégé, he look harmless."

"Who knows, he could be in training or something, or he could be his little brother, but I got a gut feeling about this one, I think we on to something."

"I'm wit you, but we can't let them see us following them," Darryle expressed, once he saw them load the last bag.

"I got dis, just lean ya seat back."

Darryle did just that, however, his thoughts ran rampant, and he has to get some clarity, "Mack, let me ask you a question?"

"Speak on it."

"I notice a lot of these racist people like liquor, what's that about?"

Mack chuckles, "Man everybody like liquor, it's not a race thing, but if you wanna get deep, liquor is considered a truth serum, it brings the true you out."

"Man, I drunk enough to know that."

"Did you?"

"Hell yeah! "

Mack nods, "So I guess you a timid little something, huh?"

Darryle balls his face up, "Hell no!"

"My point exactly! Somebody like you don't need liquor to act out, you already outspoken as it is, and you far from timid, so when you drink it don't make you noting but more worse."

"What you mean by that?"

"Man, you ain't gotta make a face, it's not like I'm shooting from the hip or nothing, you know how you get when you drink, you start tripping."

Darryle sighs, "Man, what do that got to do with anything?"

"Nothing, I'm just making a point, and you just so happen to be the example, but back to my case and point," he said, ignoring Darryle's scowl, "if you get an uptight chick that's playing games with that thing, as soon as she take a sip of that yak, she gon' loosen right the fuck up, and all that shy and uptight shit gon' go right out the door. See, the thing is, she already wanna give it up, but this persona that she tryna uphold won't allow that, that's why chicks don't like to drink around men, especially uptight ones."

"Why is that?"

"Cause they gon' take them drawers off, and when they wake up sober, guess what?"

"What?"

"They gon' cuss they self out, and swear they a slut for the rest of they life, and when they see you again, they gon' act like you never existed."

"You serious?"

"It happened to me on several occasions, but let me tell you about your history, the black man. When we was slaves back in the day, pickin cotton and shit with no shirts on in them hot ass fields, you had the uppity white women that used to sit on they porches and lust off the black man. That was the norm for them. They never saw a man with that many muscles, plus it's natural for a woman to lust when she see something different. Those punk ass white men was outta shape, with beer bellies and little cocks."

Darryle bursts out laughing, "Don't you mean dicks."

"No, I said it right the first time, white men got cocks and black men got dicks."

"That sound stereotypical."

"How? Shit, they refer to they own manhood as cocks, so I'm not stereotyping nobody, I'm just stating facts," he explained, before he looks at Darryle, "and on some real shit, when you ever hear a black man refer to they penis as a cock?" He gave Darryle all of a millisecond before he answered for him, "Never!"

Darryle chuckles, "You do got a point."

"Anyway, back to these curious white women, they would fantasize about us all the time, but they was too timid to act on it until they got drunk. When that liquor got in they system, they would tell us to fuck they brains out, something they husband couldn't do. And the very next day when they was sober, you know what?"

"What? "

"They would call us a million and one niggers, when in all actuality, they was secretly in love with this nigger di--"

Darryle doubles over in his seat laughing, "Mannn, you is a trip."

"I know, but anyway, it's time to look at a racist person that think about diabolical shit in they head. They might be timid, but when they get drunk, the real person come out. I know you heard the saying; a drunk tongue speaks a sober mind."

"Yeah, I heard that before."

"It's the truth, now let's be real for a minute, a drunk mutha fucka had to come up with the notion of dressing up in all white with a mask on. I mean, who in they right mind would actually be silly enough to walk around like that."

Darryle chuckles, "You got another point."

"I don't just got a point, I'm on point."

Darryle shakes his head, "Why you always gotta analyze everything?"

"Why is the sky blue?"

Darryle sighs, "Man, like I know."

"Exactly, some things are not meant to know."

"Slow down some Mack, it look like they driving up to that barnyard."

"I see em Blaze, just lean back in ya seat," he said, as he narrowed his e yes and killed the engine.

CHAPTER 14

"Ring, ring!"

Red's answer s his cell-phone, having already checked the caller ID, "Hey Bill, didn't me and my partner just see you, not even a hour ago?"

"Yeah," Bill whispers, "but remember that nigger problem we got, well it just got a whole lot bigger!"

Red's perks up, "What's the problem?"

"A call just came in not too long ago reporting his disappearance."

"Can't you put a lid on that shit, Bill?"

"Not on this one Red, apparently that nigger is important enough for the F.B.I. to get involved."

"F.B.I.?" Red's repeated.

"You can bet your red ass, and considering how long he's been missing, they're kicking down doors."

"Fuck!" Red's spat.

"So, what're your plans Red?"

"Hell, if I know Bill. We just pulled up to the Goddamn barn for crying out loud, and on top of that I haven't even talked to the Grand Dragon yet."

"Okay Red, I gotta go, but I'll be sure to keep you updated, and another thing, don't burn any crosses tonight, they're gonna be looking for that."

"Got it Bill." Red's ends the call.

Ryan heard bits and pieces on Red's end, and from what he could gather he knew there was a real problem, especially from the spaced out look on Red's face. "Is everything alright?" He asked, knowing it wasn't.

Red's doesn't answer right away. He rubs the sides of his temples not believing what he just heard. "Fuck!" He yells while banging on the steering wheel.

Ryan jumps in his seat, startled by the outburst.

When Red's somewhat calms down, he looks at Ryan with bloodshot eyes, and barks, "1 want you to stay in there with that nigger until tomorrow night, don't call anybody and don't leave his sight, you got that?"

"Yeah, I got it," Ryan timidly answered.

"Good," Red spat, as he unscrews the cap off a whiskey bottle, "cause you're gonna have 1ta kill that nigger before Sunday!"

CHAPTER 15

Mark could hear pacing back and forth. A few moments earlier he heard the barn door open, thus alerting him of company. At the moment he's hot, it's hard for him to breathe, and in the last four days all he had was one sandwich and enough water to keep him alive. This person, whoever it was, he could only hope had food and water.

"Hello," Mark humbly called.

Ryan stops pacing and stares at the pastor. He's never killed a human being before, and now his KKK brothers want him to kill this black man for absolutely nothing. He would surely have to be drunk for the occasion, under no circumstances could he be sober.

"Hello," the pastor called again.

"Why should I let you live?" Ryan barked.

"Because God let you live," Mark fired back.

"50! "

"Ryan, is that you?"

"Does it matter?"

"It matters to me."

Ryan snatches the pillowcase from the pastor's head, "You don't know me!" He spat, with bloodshot eyes.

"God knows you, Ryan."

He starts pacing again, frustration clear in his gait. He wishes the pastor would make him angry, so he could at least feel justified. After a moment of pondering, he stops pacing and stands directly in front of the pastor, and without warning.

"POW!" He smacks the pastor, drawing blood in the process.

Mark topples over from the force of the blow, but somehow he's able to muster enough strength to hoist himself back to his knees. While blood trickles from his lip, he stares at Ryan through pained eyes, and what he sees is a frustrated kid who has a lot of pain bottled up. "Go ahead Ryan, let it out," He egged.

Ryan stands there with his hands balled into fists, staring at the pastor wanting a reason to strike him, but he doesn't have one, so he thinks back to when he lost his parents, and that makes him angry and before he even realized it, he had his hands around the pastors neck, as tears stream down his face.

"That's... right..." Mark murmurs, through a partially closed windpipe, "let...it...out, Ryan," he manages to say.

Ryan heard him loud and clear, and he starts crying even more once he realizes what he's doing. This man is innocent, blameless, he thinks to himself. And before he knew it, he loosens his grip and hugs the pastor tight.

Tears stream down Mark's face as he speaks in Ryan's ear, "God loves you son."

"I'm sorry man... I... -"

"It's okay Ryan, I understand."

Ryan pulls back from the embrace and stares at the pastor before speaking, "Please forgive me. "

Mark smiles, "I already have son, I already have."

Ryan quickly unbinds the pastor's hands and feet, "They wanted me to kill you tomorrow, but I just can't do it, I have to let you go."

"It's okay Ryan, you've been touched by God."

"I think I have too because my conscious wouldn't allow me to harm you."

"That was God Ryan, and God is good."

"I believe he is," Ryan then looks around, "Im'a go and make sure it's clear out there and when I come back, be ready."

"Okay, but before you go, I would like to introduce Jesus into your life."

"How?"

"Repeat after me."

"Okay."

"Lord Jesus, I invite you into my life. I believe you died for me and that your blood pays for my sins and provides me with the gift of eternal life. By faith, I receive that gift, and I acknowledge you as my Lord and Savior. Amen."

After Ryan repeated everything the pastor said, he opens his eyes and hugs the pastor for a second time, "Thank you, man, for doing this for me."

"It's okay Ryan, God welcomes all his people, you are now saved and it's your duty to spread the word."

"I will," a revamped Ryan said, "now let me go out here to make sure nobody's around, I wanna get you out of here safe."

"God willing."

Ryan nods before he heads to the entrance. He turns around one more time and smiles at the pastor, who in turn smiles back. He then opens the door and hastily closes it back.

"Click, clack! Where the fuck you think you gon' cracka!" An angry black man spat, with a big gun shoved in Ryan's face.

CHAPTER 16

The F.B.I. has formed a special tactics team assigned to the disappearance of the political preacher, Mark Goodman. Since they were notified of this event, they've been hard at work. Special agent, Michael Fuller, is the lead investigator in charge and at the moment he's in F.B.I. Headquarters growing gray hairs by the second.

"Goddamit John," he spat at his underling, "we got less than forty-eight hours to find this man, but he's already been missing for four freakin days!" He used his fingers to sift through his orange frizzled hair that sits no higher than two inches on his head. He's a white male in his mid-forties, and ever since he left the army he always sported a bold cut with a clean shaven face, however, he's as pale as a prisoner who hasn't seen the sun in ages.

"Yeah Mike," his underling agrees, "His family was too scared to notify the police because they were warned that if they did, the pastor would die."

Agent Fuller scratched the side of his head at that, "Yeah well, I got a hunch on that one too. Being as though we're dealing with the KKK in that predominantly racist area, I wouldn't be surprised if half of the police force were active KKK members. As a matter of fact," he said, taking a seat at an empty computer and typing several keys, "How many racist cults do we have in that area?"

"I believe it's a little over forty sir."

"Alright then, within a 100-mile radius of that church, I want satellite surveillance cued in. Anything burning, any suspicious groups of individuals wearing white KKK robes, anything, and I mean anything, you notify me." Agent Fuller then stands to his feet to address his tactic team, of twenty well-trained individuals. They're dressed in all black tactical uniforms, with F.B.I. scrawled on the fabric. "People," he barks, "we literally have 40 hours to find Mark Goodman, if he isn't already dead, and he's more than likely holed up somewhere waiting to die. We're dealing with the KKK here, so I'm almost certain they're planning some type of ritual for his death. You all have pictures of the pastor, so make sure you keep a keen eye open for any suspicious activity, let's move out men!"

CHAPTER 17

Darryle has the timid white kid gripped up by the collar of his shirt, with the gun inches away from his face. Ryan is scared shitless, as Darryle barks his next order, "We gon' walk back in that barn and you gon' keep ya mouth shut, you follow?"

"Ye…ye…yes man," Ryan stutters, "please, don't ki… kill… me. "

"Shut the fuck up!" Mack barked, "Who else in there with you?"

"It's… jus, one…other…person sir."

"Does he have a gun?" Mack hissed.

"N, n, no, sir."

"Okay," Darryle says, "you gon' slowly open that door, and if so much as a bird fly out, I'm gon' pull this trigger."

"O… ok… -"

"Shut up fool, and open that damn door!" Darryle spat, "I'm tired of hearing ya stuttering ass!" He aggressively spins Ryan toward the door, with the gun trained on the back of his head. As soon as Ryan grabs the knob, Darryle whispers in his ear, "Turn that knob real slow, ya hear?"

Ryan nods, as he slowly opens the door. The barn is dark and unpleasantly damp as a putrid odor permeates the air.

Both Mack and Darryle contort their noses, "Damn man," Mack barks, "what the fuck you done kilt!"

"No... no... nothing... m... man, I swear."

"Ryan, is that you?" Mark called from the shadows.

"Ye... -"

"Shut the fuck up!" Mack spat at Ryan, "show yourself or I'ma start shooting."

"There's no need for violence," Mark soothes, as he steps in clear view with his hands in the air.

"Oh shit!" Mack whispers, "That's your pops, man!"

Once Darryle sees his father he has a mix of emotions. His dad, who's usually well-groomed and sharply dressed, looks like a homeless bum who saw better days. His head, which is usually razor bald, now has hair, only growing on the sides and back, leaving the top hairless. His beard is awfully fuzzy, with visible lint balls. His face is noticeably dirty, making him a shade darker than his normal mocha complexion. His once blue suit is wrinkled something fierce, along with his shirt underneath, which used to be white. It has visible blood stains along with compacted dirt. Darryle is speechless, and as he continues to look at his father, he realizes that he's lost a lot of weight as well.

Darryle abruptly glares at Ryan, who still has his hands in the air. "Crack!" Darryle smacks him with the butt of the gun sending him dizzy to the floor.

"Please man, don't hurt me," Ryan shrieks, while in the fetal position, this time without the lisp.

Darryle jumps on top of Ryan and begins to pistol whip him mercilessly.

Mark sees the assault, and out of pure instinct he rushes to Ryan's aid, unaware that it's his own son. He tackles Darryle to the surface, and pleads for Ryan's life, "Don't hurt him, man, it's me you want," he managed to get out, as he has Darryle bear hugged from behind.

"Let me go pop, Im'a kill that cracka!" Darryle spat.

"Son, is that you?" Mark asked, semi loosening his grip.

"Yeah, it's me! Now let me go so I can kill that cracka!"

"Boy you need to calm down," His dad firmly spat.

Darryle heaves out a long sigh, "Pop, Im'a ask you one more time, let, me, the, fuck, go!" He pronounced every word.

"Or what!" Mark barks, "you gon' kill me?" He tightens his grip.

"Man, get ya fuckin hands-"

"Boy!" Mark shouts at his son, "I brought yo black ass in this world and I'll' surely take you out of it!"

"Fuck you!" Darryle spat.

After that, both son and father wrestled on the ground as if they were strangers. Although Mark was weak, he handled his son with ease, as he kept gaining the upper hand. Mack, on the other hand, didn't know what to do, he definitely knew one thing, and he wasn't breaking this bout up. He never saw Pastor Mark lose his cool like that, but when it comes to Darryle, he clearly understood, and although that was his gang brother, he secretly hoped Darryle would lose, and then maybe he would learn some respect.

During the dispute, Ryan tries to creep off, until Mack sees him.

"You take another step, and Im'a blow yo shit clean off.

Ryan nods and places his hands back in the air.

In the mud, both Mark and Darryle are still going at it, until Mark puts his son in a choke hold. With Mark on his son's back who continues to writhe, he begins to breathlessly speak, "Are you done?" He asked.

Darryle remains quiet.

"I'm not letting you go until you surrender!"

Darryle still remains quiet.

"God loves you, son, it's time for you to get saved before it's too late." Mark then looks at Mack, who still has his gun trained on Ryan, "What's your name?"

"Who me?" Mack questions.

"Yeah you!"

"Um, they call me Mack."

"Okay Mack, grab that gun that my son dropped and throw it over there," Mark pointed toward the back of the barn.

Mack picks Darryle's gun up. However, he becomes hesitant, "I'll just hold it, Pastor Mark. I don't think it would be a good idea to toss it."

"Mack, do you believe in God?"

"Somewhat."

"Alright Mack, I want you to listen to what I'm about to say," he said, still holding his son, "No weapon formed against you shall prosper, and any tongue that rises against you in judgement, you shall condemn. This is the heritage of the servants of the Lord, and their vindication from me, says the Lord. Now throw that gun, Mack, along with yours, and come over here to put hands on your friend."

Mack is still skeptical, so he only tosses the gun a few feet away, before walking towards Pastor Mark.

"Go on Mack," Mark coaxes, "put your hand on his arm."

Mack kneels down on one knee and places a hand on Darryle's arm, unsure of the Pastor's plan.

"Come on over here Ryan, I need you too."

Ryan complies with no questions asked, and right before Mark begins to pray, the barn door bursts open.

CHAPTER 18

"Mom, what did they say?" Mariam asked.

Carylon sighs before helping herself to a seat. " They basically wanted to know how long he was missing, and once I told them, they became irate."

"Did you tell them why it took you so long to contact them?" Samson asked.

"Yeah, I sure did."

Both Mariam and Samson stare at their mother, "And?" They both say.

"That was basically it, they kinda got quiet after that, and then this other guy came on the line, stating he was with the F.B.I."

"That should be good, right?" Mariam asks Samson.

"I would think so," he offered, "what else did he say, mom? "

"He asked me some routine questions about your father's church, what did he have on that day, was anything different about his behavior. I mean this guy asked me some real odd questions."

"Well mom, he's with the F.B.I. so you know they're trained in that field." Samson explained.

"I can imagine, he say he the lead investigator."

Both Mariam and Samson become hopeful, "Then I know he's good, I done saw enough movies to know that much." Mariam quips.

"Did he say anything else?"

Carylon sighs again before she answers her son, "Yeah, he said for me to stay here to see if they call back and if they do he want me to keep them on the phone as long as I can."

"Yeah, he's good," Samson acknowledges, "he probably has the phone tapped."

"Have any of y'all seen or heard from your brother?" Carylon inquired.

"Not since that day he came in here tripping," Mariam said.

"He probably out spray painting a wall or something, you know he got issues, Mom."

"He's still your brother Samson," His mother reminds him.

"He sure don't act like it."

"Samson!" Carylon spat as if he should know better, "Your brother loves you dearly, now he might have a funny way of showing it, but he does love you." Carylon rubs her temples, "I been so concerned about your father, I haven't thought twice about Darryle. "

"Mom, I'm sure he's fine," Mariam adds.

"I'm sure he is too, but just to be even surer, let's all hold hands and bow our heads."

CHAPTER 19

"Lookee what we got here," Red's spat, with several of his KKK buddies in tow. There are three of them, including Red's and they're all standing in the doorway with AR-15 assault rifles trained on the circle.

Mack tries to ease toward his gun, already cursing himself for tossing it.

"You take another step nigger, and Im'a blow your nigger brains all over this barn!" Red's spat, glaring at Mack. "Ryan," he calls, "you alright kid?"

Ryan quickly moves away from the trio, "No, they broke in here to free the pastor, and they were gonna kill me."

"Come on over here."

Ryan runs to Red.

"Which one of them niggers did that to your face?" Red's hissed.

Ryan doesn't hesitate, as he points at Darryle.

"Johnny," Red's barks at his cohort, "grab that nigger and bring his ass here."

Mark jumps in front of his son with his arms outstretched, "Please sir, take me ins-"

"CRACK!" Johnny smashes the butt of the heavy rifle into the pastor's face, instantly knocking him out. And before

Mack grows any bright ideas, Johnny goes over the top of his head as well, just for good measure, knocking him out in the process.

Johnny aims the assault rifle at Darryle, who by now has his hands covering his face, scared to death.

Red's looks to his other cohort, "Steve, go over there and help Johnny string that nigger up, we gon' give his ass an old fashion slave beating."

Steve chuckles, "My pleasure."

Red's then addresses Ryan, "You, go over there and tie those sleeping monkeys up. I don't want them to miss the action."

Ryan does as he's told and by the time he finishes that task, he peers over and sees Darryle butt naked, tied up with rope bound by his wrists, hanging from a high beam. His ankles are tied to the lower beams, as he's stretched out in the form of an X.

Red's steps in front of Darryle, and he has to look up at him, considering his elevated dilemma. "So," he begins, "you like to put your hands on white men, huh?" Red's spat at a visibly scared Darryle, "We gon beat you to death boy, you know that!" He continued before he spit out a thick glob of chew.

Tears sprang from Darryle's eyes. This white man who Mack had said was a certified racist was definitely the truth, and for some reason, he believed every threat he just made. Please, God, spare my life, he silently prayed.

"Johnny," Red's barked, "grab enough horse reins foe us all, I think we got a runaway slave on our hands."

Everyone with the exception of Ryan and the victims burst out laughing. Moments later, Johnny returns with the reins and passes each of his cohorts a set.

"This what I'm talking about right here boys!" Red's says, clearly overjoyed as he caresses the thick dusty leather rein. He then takes several steps back away from Darryle, studying his bare back. He whips his arm in the air and strikes Darryle on the shoulder blade.

"PAP! Yee ha!" Red's yells, as if he's riding a horse.

Once the pain registers, Darryle screams out in agony. His cries are so loud, it wakes up Mack and Mark from their unconscious state.

"Come on boys," Red's sings, "let's ride this here nigger horse."

Red's along with Johnny and Steve, beat Darryle for every bit of 15 minutes. Darryle is in so much pain, he can no longer scream. His back is bleeding profusely as well as his buttock and thighs. His father along with Mack are literally crying for the pain they know he's enduring. This is surely the devil's work.

Out of breath, Red's peers at his blood soaked reins before he breaks out with a sinister smile, "Good job boys," he says to his 2 cohorts, "that'll teach his ass a good ole lesson."

"You got that right," Steve joins in.

Red's glances at his watch, "Sorry boys," he addresses a bound Mack and Mark, "around this time tomorrow, you niggers a be on your way to nigger paradise."

"We not gon' kill em tonight?" An anxious Johnny inquires.

"Fraid not there Johnny," Red's admits, "we gotta rally here tomorrow," he looks at his watch again, "well actually tonight, I didn't known we were foolin around wit these here niggers for dis long. Anyhow, I'm bout to contact the Grand Dragon and fill him in on the good news, we bout to have ourselves a nigger bar-b-que. Johnny, I want you to come wit me, Steve, you stay here with Ryan and watch these niggers. If they so much as break wind, you know what to do."

Steve smiles, displaying a mouth full of chew decayed teeth, "What about this one here, Red?" He points to a strung up Darryle, "should I leave em like that?"

Red's becomes thoughtful as he peers at Darryle. He sees blood streaming down his naked body, slowly dripping from his bare feet and he doesn't think twice, "Leave his ass up there, by the time I get back he'll be half dead."

CHAPTER 20

Less than 24 hours to live

Darryle begins to stir from his unconscious state. He was beaten so bad he passed out from the pain. His body feels numb, and as he's hung up, he moans out in agonizing discomfort.

"Son," Mark calls out, "you hear me?" He whispers as he and Mack are bound by chains, directly in front of Darryle. It's now six hours after the beating and Mark's been praying ever since. Dry tear stains streak down his face as he looks at his son through pained eyes. He would've given up anything in the world to trade places with his son. He starts to cry even now, thinking about the punishment his son received.

Mack, on the other hand, has been quiet throughout the whole ordeal. He only wished he would've followed his instincts and kept those guns in his palms. At least they would've had a fighting chance. He then peers at Steve and Ryan across the room. Steve is snoring against the barn's shed as he sits on a handmade hay mound. He has the assault rifle draped around his neck from the strap, as the gun is loosely dangling from his hip. What he wouldn't give to have his hands on that gun right now. He would first shoot Ryan's punk ass, who at the moment appears to be sleeping alongside his racist cronies.

"Dad," Darryle moans out.

Mark perks up, "I'm here son, I'm here," he soothes.

"I'm sorry dad! I really am," he cries, "I don't want to die like this Dad, please!" He begged.

Mark can't help it as the tears come. He never in his life saw or heard his son in so much agony, and there's not a damn thing he can do. "Son, it's alright, we'll get through this!"

"Please, dad!" He moans out again, "help me. Please!"

Mack starts to cry as well. His friend is in so much pain he can literally hear the ache in his voice, and at the moment he comes to the same conclusion as Darryle.

"Dad!" He pleads, "I can't bear it, it hurts so bad!"

"It's okay son, God doesn't put nothing on us that we can't bear. Do you believe that son?"

"Yes I do," he moans, "I just don't want to die, dad, not like this."

"I know son, I know. But God hears you son and he knows your heart."

Darryle starts really crying, not so much from the pain but more so of the fact that he never gave God a chance, and now in this tumultuous moment, God is the first name he calls. "Do you think he'll forgive me?" He cried.

At that exact moment, Mark sees a new Darryle. He sees his curious baby boy who was 5 years old getting into trouble. He even hears his baby boy, the son he loved so much. The son that asked about God that loved church and was always curious about the angels. This tragedy is about to bring God back into his son's life.

Mark can remember so many years ago, when he sat Darryle on his lap, and his son said to him, "I don' t want to go to hell," and Mark told him the exact same thing he's about to tell him now, "Repeat after me son."

CHAPTER 21

F.B.I. Headquarters

"Sir, you're not gonna believe this," John, the underling said to Agent Fuller.

"What is it, John?" Agent Fuller spat.

"Well, a 9-11 call came in over ten minutes ago and the caller doesn't say a word, he simply keeps the phone on, and we're now getting a live feed of what appears to be our Pastor."

Agent Fuller jumps out of his seat and storms over to John's computer, "Turn it up, John!" He barked.

John complies, and through the advanced technology, this is heard, "Lord Jesus I invite you into my life." Mark says.

"Lord Jesus I invite you into my life," Two voices repeat.

"I believe you died for me and that your blood pays for my sins and provides me with the gift of eternal life," Mark said.

"I believe you died for me and that your blood pays for my sins ·and provides me with the gift of eternal life." The two voices repeat.

"By faith I receive that gift, and I acknowledge you as my Lord and Savior. Amen." Mark finished.

"By faith I receive that gift, and I acknowledge you as my Lord and Savior. Amen." The two voices repeated.

"You are now saved," Mark says, "you too Mack."

"Thank you, Pastor," A voice says.

"Thank you, dad," A distressed voice seconds.

Agent Fuller bangs on the desk, "We got 'em!" He then looks at John, "get me a location on that feed."

"Right away sir." He said while typing away, and several seconds later he gets a location, "Got it, sir."

Agent Fuller stoops down and peers at the computer screen, "I'll be damned, that's damn near in the woods, way out in the country."

John types some more, "Sir, it's directly inside of a barnhouse."

Agent Fuller becomes thoughtful, "Find out who that feed is coming from and tell me everything about this person, in God's speed!"

John doesn't answer, he simply types away, and within a matter of seconds, any and everything pertaining to that cell-phone pops up. "Sir, this phone is registered to a Ryan Banks, his family recently died in a car crash two years ago, he was raised on a farm, and he lives on the internet. His most frequent searches are…" John types for several more seconds, "White Supremacy!"

"BINGO!" Agent Fuller shouts. He then glances at his watch, before throwing on his F.B.I. vest, "Radio that location to all units, pronto. I also want a chopper on this, we got less than 2 hours, and if we're lucky, we might catch these racist pricks in the act!"

CHAPTER 22

The night is alive as the stars twinkle in the sky. Twenty-one Clan members occupy this deserted farm in the middle of nowhere. A light breeze careens through the air as all members are dressed in their traditional KKK robes, with the exception of the Grand Dragon, who has on a blue robe. They're all joined together in a wide circle, and directly in the center stands four wooden crosses.

Each cross is mounted into the earth as they stand sturdy, having recently been drenched in gasoline. Among the crosses, three of them are occupied with human bodies. Mark is tied to one, as well as his son and Mack. The fourth cross is slightly bigger than the occupied three. It stands 5 feet in front of the three adjoining crosses,

"What a beautiful night!" The Grand Dragon shouts.

The group cheers him on as they hail loud obscenities.

"Today my people, we will be one step closer. These niggers have plagued our existence long enough, I tell you all. The time has come," He raises his voice, "to where the line gets drawn." He pauses for effect, as he slowly looks at everyone, "These niggers will no longer be allowed to sit on a bus, let alone in the back of one!" More cheers erupt at his obvious rhetoric, "They won't be able to breathe our air, or walk in our parks! Since they got that nigger, President, they want to make demands now. They want our police to wear body cams, they want us to take our flag down, our Confederate flag!" He then lights his torch, "What has America come to people? They want this to be the land of the free! He literally starts screaming, "But I'm here to tell you, this will never be the land of the free! This is the land of White Supremacy, and this land will soon be nigger free!" He screamed at the top of his lungs.

All of his followers are really riled up now, and their cheers can be heard miles away.

The Grand Dragon takes the torch and walks to the lone cross. As soon as the fire touches it, it bursts into flames. He then takes several steps back and throws his hands in the air. This gesture only draws more cheers and rants. "Ryan!" He shouts, "Step forward to bear this torch! "

At this point, Mark is praying hard, Darryle is crying his eyes out and Mack is simply praying for a quick death. As each of them is tied to their own cross, they are all to their own thoughts.

A continuous rant is nonstop until a loud thunder erupts. The thundering was so loud, it actually sounded as if the sky cracked in half. It made everyone present jump.

The rants are no more, as it grows eerily quiet. The only sound that can be heard is the cackling from the burning lumber.

Ryan is stuck in his tracks, and only halfway toward the Grand Dragon he wonders, this must be a sign from God. Right after that thought another rumble sounds off in the heavens, spurring every pair of seeing eyes to look in the sky. The roar seemed everlasting until the surging rain pelts reaches it's destination. The heavy downpour quickly washed the once burning flame that caressed the cross, along with the hand held torch that loosely dangled from Ryan's grasp.

In succession to this, helicopter wings ensue. Then as if a stadium was just opening, bright lights are activated, one by one, covering the entire melee. Followed by this, footsteps and heavy artillery can be heard closing the distance, and before any of the Clan had a chance,

"Freeze! This is the F.B.I. You are all under arrest!" Was shouted through a bullhorn.

Every member lay face down on the drenched grass, as they are each handcuffed and carted off.

THE END

EPILOGUE

After all was said and done the entire Clan received twenty years in the Federal Penitentiary, besides Ryan and the Grand Dragon. The Grand Dragon was sentenced to thirty years under the R.I.C.O. ACT.

Ryan received probation for his cooperation and subsequent role in helping to bring this racist cult to justice. He is now a dedicated and devoted church member at Pastor Mark's church. He also started a movement called "I DENOUNCE HATE" all over South Carolina, which is quickly growing throughout the Country.

Mack is no longer gang affiliated and is now a history teacher at a local public school. Every Sunday he attends Pastor Mark's church and gives thanks to God for sparing his life. He is currently dating a white woman.

Darryle has enrolled back in school and is months away from earning his diploma. He's also back in the church and he's now a piano player. He no longer lives the gang life and tours the neighborhood to spread the word of God. His life has done a 360 turn around and everyday he thanks God for sparing his life.

Pastor Mark is back to running his church and he now has more members than ever. He's also running for Mayor and as it stands he's ahead in the polls by a landslide. He's expecting another child from his lovely wife Carylon, and he continues to spread the word of God down South.

A WORD FROM THE AUTHOR

Hate is a powerful word, but love is more powerful. We as a people, no matter the ethnicity, must denounce hate. It has no place in our society! When I saw this awful tragedy that occurred in Charleston, I cried several times. This act of violence simply because of the color of one's skin made me think, why! Is this what society has come to? Do we slaughter another race because of the color of their skin? Or the belief in their religion? Has the value of human life decreased, as the dollar amount of our money in the next country? The two must, can't, and shall not be compared. Life is what matters, not one's race.

No offense but we are not a third world Country. These acts of violence because of race and hate must be denounced. Whenever hate and racism take place, the spirit of condemnation festers in need of a catalyst. We as one people must be that catalyst. As I close, my condolences go out to those families, and may all 9 Charleston victims rest in peace.

Your Author,
William J.

     I DENOUNCE HATE!

ABOUT THE AUTHOR

William J is a new author. He was born and raised in Philadelphia, PA. As an adolescent he loved to read books. His mother always told him that he was very gifted and could accomplish anything he put his mind to. He recently opened up one of his gifts, and is continually striving to become a brand name author. Besides writing, he loves sports, computers, drawing, and life itself. At this very moment, his genre is urban fiction, but he plans to expand in the future.

His life experience, imagination and lessons learned have crafted his writing that many will enjoy.

His New Trilogy – BRINK will be released in 2018.

WILLIAM'S CONTACT INFORMATION

William J can be reached at the following locations!

Facebook/Twitter/GoodReads/YouTube

Sign up for William J's:
Mailing List: http://eepurl.com/bpcPyv
Text Alerts: http://clk2.it/Rm0BNn

AZINA MEDIA
C/O: William J
237 Flatbush Avenue, #187
Brooklyn, NY 11217